Bradwell's Book of

The Peak District

a Feast of **Fun, Facts** and **History!**

Published by Bradwell Books
11 Orgreave Close Sheffield S13 9NP
Email: books@bradwellbooks.co.uk

Compiled by Camilla Zajac

Excerpts from:

DERBYSHIRE DIALECT – Mike Smith

DERBYSHIRE MURDER STORIES – David Bell

DERBYSHIRE GHOST STORIES – Jill Armitage

DERBYSHIRE RECIPES – Amanda Wragg

All rights reserved. No part of this publication may be reproduced, stored in a retrieval system or transmitted in any form or by any means, electronic, mechanical, photocopying, recording or otherwise without the prior permission of Bradwell Books.

British Library Cataloguing in Publication Data:
a catalogue record for this book is available from the British Library.

1st Edition

ISBN: 9781912060573

Designed and Typeset by: Andrew Caffrey

Print: Gomer Press, Llandysul, Ceredigion SA44 4JL

Cover Images Credits: Main: Andrew & Susan Caffrey
Left to right. iStock, iStock, Bakewell Pudding Shop, Creative Commons, Andrew & Susan Caffrey, iStock

Bradwell's Book of The Peak District

a Feast of Fun, Facts and History!

BRADWELL BOOKS

Contents

INTRODUCTION
Introducing the Peak District, the UK's first national park, a place that can be both bleak and cosy and which boasts a history as rich as its varied landscape and an appeal to visitors going back centuries.

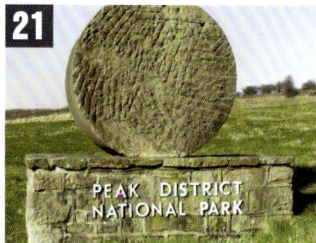

DERBYSHIRE DIALECT
Explore the words and phrases which you can hear in and around the Peak District and the clues they reveal about its rich past.

WIT AND HUMOUR
From entertaining one-liners to rib-tickling tales, enjoy some humour based in and around the Peak District!

HISTORY
Discover how the Peak District became the first of Britain's national parks, why an entire village was once moved, and more.

GHOST STORIES
The Peak District boasts quite a collection of otherworldly visitors, from the strange figures seen at Calke Abbey to the peculiar powers of the screaming skull of Tunstead Farm. Read on for some creepy tales from the Peaks!

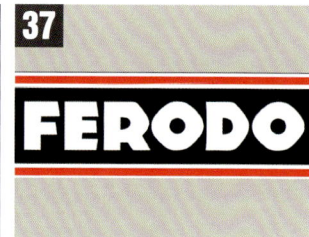

LOCAL NAMES
We have much to thank the Peak District for. Not only for being an incredible place to visit and stay, but also for its contribution to everyday life, from the first collapsible umbrella to a well-known way to clean greasy hands!

MYTHS AND LEGENDS
Believe it or not, but the landlocked Peak District is said to be home to not one but two mermaids! Watch out also for the mysterious and powerful Stones of Mouselow and the area's connection with Robin Hood and Little John.

SPORT
We all know that the peaks are a popular destination for outdoor activities like walking and climbing, but what about the area's fascinating tradition of Shrovetide football? Read on to find out more.

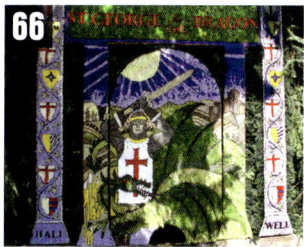

CUSTOMS
Find out about the enduring Peak District custom of well dressing and why it is that traditions featuring flowers, both paper and real, have such a significance in the area.

MURDER STORIES
From a tragic duel to the terrible treatment of two young lovers, brace yourself for real-life stories of murder in the Peak District.

LOCAL RECIPES
The Peak District is known for its famous pudding. Just don't call it a tart! In this section, you can learn how to make that pudding and other traditional dishes.

FAMOUS LOCALS
Locals from in and around the Peak District have made their mark on science, culture, literature and TV. From a fashion icon to James Bond, get to know the locals who have done their home towns and villages proud!

Introduction

IT TAKES A LIFETIME TO TRULY GET TO KNOW THE PEAK DISTRICT. NO WONDER, WHEN IT COVERS SUCH A VAST AND VARIED AREA, REACHING ACROSS NO FEWER THAN FIVE COUNTIES.

Divided between the Dark Peak in the north and the White Peak in the south, this is a place of contrasts.

Not only is it a home to many people, and an area with thriving farms and businesses, but it is also the site of one of the best-loved national parks in the world. The Peak District is full of picturesque views in rural areas such as KINDER SCOUT, DOVEDALE and around MAM TOR, but it also has its cosy, quintessentially English *'villagey'* feel in places such as BUXTON, MATLOCK and LONGNOR. While it is the home of the Bakewell Pudding, it also contains 2,900 listed buildings.

The name is deceptive. There are no real peaks in the Peak District. But there is pretty much everything else. From open moorland to rivers to woodlands as beautiful as they are ancient and grasslands of international importance, you could take a walk every day in the Peak District and discover something new each time you go. It is an ancient place and packed full of clues to its past. This is the place where an entire village was moved on the whim of an aristocrat and where you can still catch a glimpse in dryer weather of villages that were submerged long ago to make way for reservoirs. This is a place of traditions, from the well dressing that continues to this day to the custom of sharing a special message through flowers. In DOVEDALE, you will also find clues to the fascinating custom of pushing coins into the bark of a tree. If you happen to notice twisted or flattened coins sticking out of a tree bark, it's not fairies but an ancient local custom.

The Peak District is also a place where ancient tales of a screaming skull and a set of weird, inscribed stones with magical powers still cause shivers down the spine. It is the location of the famous plague village, the home of a brave group of people who sacrificed themselves to prevent the spread of the deadly infection. It is also where the Lady of the Lamp grew up and where ROBIN HOOD's right-hand man is said to be buried.

While it is visited by more than ten million people every year, the Peak District turns out to have been a big draw for many centuries. This has been proven by various archaeological finds and features which make up a huge part of the landscape's character, from barrows at MARGERY HILL to henges like the NINE LADIES STONE CIRCLE at STANTON MOOR. Escaping to the Peak District for some relaxation is not a new thing. Tourists were heading to the area as far back as the 1600s! This attraction is also part of the challenge for the Peak District – how to continue to welcome tourists while protecting the beautiful landscape and cultural heritage such as drystone walls and listed buildings from the damage caused by cars and footfall.

Let's hope that the popularity of the Peak District helps to preserve rather than endanger its many beautiful features. Because this is a fascinating

Millstones - iStock

and special part of the world – a place that brings us closer to our past while providing solace and comfort from the demands of modern life. Its accessibility is part of its magic, but also part of the risk to its survival. While its landscape and features are diverse, the pleasure it brings many people is consistent. Let's hope it stays that way for good. Of course, this little book can only provide a brief insight into some of this area's most fascinating aspects. But hopefully it offers a taste of what there is to discover in the Peak District.

HISTORY

A Popular Destination

Did you know that the Peak District National Park was the very first of Britain's 15 national parks?

Founded in 1951, it covers an area of 555 square miles (1,438 sq. km), reaching into no fewer than five counties: DERBYSHIRE, CHESHIRE, STAFFORDSHIRE, YORKSHIRE and GREATER MANCHESTER. While it has 38,000 residents, the Peak District is visited by over 10 million visitors a year, making it one of the most popular national parks in the UK! One of the many things that make the Peak District so special is that its central location makes it easily accessible.

In fact, around 20 million people live within one hour's journey of the Peak District, while over 50 million people live within four hours' journey of it. Not only is the Peak District relatively easy to reach, but it is fairly easy to travel across, having 1,600 miles of public rights of way, including 64 miles accessible to disabled people.

The national park boasts 65 miles of off-road dedicated cycling and walking trails. It also features 34 miles of disused railways: HIGH PEAK TRAIL, TISSINGTON TRAIL and MONSAL TRAIL. Around 200 square miles (520 sq. km) is open access land, so walkers can enjoy it freely without having to stick to the paths.

Castleton - iStock

Britain's Oldest National Walking Trail

The Peak District is home to Britain's oldest long-distance national walking trail, THE PENNINE WAY, which starts in Edale. Completed in 1965, it covers 268 miles (429km), all the way from the Nag's Head Pub in EDALE to the Border Hotel in KIRK YETHOLM, Scotland.

The Dark Peak and the White Peak

The Peak District's name strongly suggests a landscape marked by mountains. But there are none. The 'Peak' of the name is actually thought have been derived from the *Pecsaetan*, an Anglo-Saxon tribe which settled in the area. While there are no actual peaks, there are many impressive features which have made the Peak District hugely popular with anyone

who loves a good view. The Dark Peak is made up of gritstone edges while the White Peak is made up of limestone dales. The highest point is the much-loved KINDER SCOUT which rises to 2,086 feet (636 metres). The deepest of the Peak District's caves is TITAN SHAFT at Castleton which is 464 feet (141.5m) high, making it taller than the London Eye! This impressive cave is the largest-known shaft of any cave in the British Isles and was discovered as recently as 1999.

RICH IN RESOURCES

As well as impressive caves, the Peak District includes 196 square miles of moorland, made up of rolling hills and farmland in the south-west Peak. It also has rich resources with caverns famed for rare BLUE JOHN stone (read more about this in the dialect section), 5,440 miles (8,750km) of drystone wall and 55 reservoirs supplying 450 million litres of water a day! More than a third of the national park is designated as Sites of Special Scientific Interest (SSSI).

A HARD-WORKING PLACE

The Peak District may look picturesque, but it is a very hard-working place. In fact, almost 90 per cent of the national park is farmland, with around 1,800 farms. Other industries include quarrying and manufacturing. Quarrying was once such a big industry in the area that the area has some 70 active and disused quarry sites – more than all other UK national parks put together! This is thanks to the area's rich mineral resources and easily accessible location. Just a small number of quarries remain open today.

Of course, the other way that locals earn their living is by benefiting from the huge numbers of tourists drawn to the place. Visitors to the area enjoy a wide range of leisure activities, from walking to climbing and from gliding to just enjoying a nice cup of tea and a Bakewell Pudding in one of the area's many tea rooms. Another hugely popular activity in the Peak District is to visit the area's beautiful listed buildings, which include CHATSWORTH HOUSE, HADDON HALL and PEVERIL CASTLE. There are an impressive 2,900 listed structures in the Peak District, ranging from farm buildings to the medieval bridge at Bakewell. The area also boasts over 450 scheduled historic monuments.

THE POWER OF A PUDDING

Dating all the way back to medieval times, pretty Bakewell is closely associated with the Peak District's history as a national park. When the area became a park, BAKEWELL was chosen to be its administrative centre. But of course Bakewell is also famous for another reason – its pudding!

The history of the making of the first Bakewell Pudding (no one in Derbyshire would ever dream of calling it Bakewell Tart!) is a classic tale of a recipe created by chance. The story goes that a group of noblemen who were visiting the WHITE HORSE INN in Bakewell (now the RUTLAND ARMS HOTEL) asked if they could be served a strawberry tart for pudding. The cook misunderstood the instructions given to her by the mistress of the hotel and spread egg mixture on top of the jam, rather than stirring it into the pastry. Instead of attracting complaints from the diners, the accidental dish was an instant hit.

MRS WILSON, the wife of a Bakewell candle-maker, acquired the recipe for the new pudding and immediately realised its commercial possibilities. She began selling the delicacy from

Bakewell Pudding - iStock

her husband's candle shop and claimed that it contained a secret ingredient known only to herself. Mrs Wilson knew that her clever ploy was working a treat when she noticed that her customers were much more inclined to wax lyrical about her puddings than about her husband's candles. The shop was transformed into the Bakewell Pudding Shop and began to attract customers from far and wide. The Old Original Bakewell Pudding Shop is still a magnet for visitors to the town, although it has now been joined by some other shops claiming to have unique access to the original recipe. But, no matter: there is a spirit of cooperation among Bakewell's shopkeepers and all are happy to cash in on the fame of a pudding that was born in the town as the result of a happy accident.

Flittin' in En'sor

Flittin' (moving) took on a whole new meaning when the entire village of Edensor (pronounced En'sor) was moved to a new location.

The demolition began in 1762, when the Fourth Duke of Devonshire decided that the view of his estate from Chatsworth House was being rudely interrupted by the sight of Edensor's rustic buildings.

The Duke began demolishing the cottages that were closest to the house, and the removal of the remaining buildings was completed by the Sixth Duke in the 1830s, when he asked his head gardener Joseph Paxton and the Derby architect John Robertson to design a new village in a location that would not be visible from the house.

Legend has it that Robertson arrived at Chatsworth with a portfolio containing all his different house designs and asked the Duke to select the one he preferred. As he was too busy at the time to make a carefully considered choice, the Duke flicked through the drawings and simply ordered one of each. As a result, every house in Edensor is different. They range in style from a castellated tower house to an Alpine-style chalet. Just one house from the original Edensor has remained in place. It sits in a dip outside the new village and was spared because it was the only cottage that could not be seen from Chatsworth House.

It's all done by Gravity

In 1797, the limestone quarries at Dove Holes were linked to the Bugsworth Canal Basin by one of the country's earliest tramways. Horses were used to pull the loaded wagons along the flatter stretches but a revolutionary gravitational railway was employed on the steepest stretch below Top o' th' Plane (the top of the incline). Loaded wagons on the down-line were connected by a hemp rope (later replaced by a chain) to empty wagons on the up-line, allowing the weight of the loaded wagons to pull the empty wagons up the hill.

Braking of the descending wagons was achieved in a rather alarming way: a brakeman would ride on the edge of the chassis and lock the wheels by leaning over and thrusting a pin into a socket between the spokes. In his biography of Joe Marchington ('Chuckling Joe'), a man who lived in the High Peak from 1873 to 1949, Crichton Porteous reports Joe's observation of these brave brakemen: *'It were great t'a watch them, they could do it like snuff.'*

How did The Peak District become a National Park?

It is all too easy to take the Peak District for granted. But it is only relatively recently that it became a national park.

The park owes its existence to the growing interest in walking in the countryside. In the 1880s, a Member of Parliament started to campaign for public access to the countryside. By the early 1900s, the public was seeking the freedom to explore the countryside and escape from built-up urban areas. This increase in visitors led to clashes with landowners, who were concerned about people walking freely around their estates. While the government made some recommendations about designating national parks, no specific progress was made, and the public grew even more discontented. This led to the events of 1932, in which a mass trespass on KINDER SCOUT saw walkers marching onto the privately owned land, where they were confronted by gamekeepers. Five of these trespassers ended up in prison. Finally, in 1936,

LOCAL **HISTORY**

a voluntary Standing Committee on National Parks was formed to argue the case for national parks and to lobby the government.

By the 1940s, the national park principle was established. After the end of the Second World War, the government set up committees to examine long-term land use. Thankfully, the preservation of nature was part of the post-war reconstruction effort. Two reports paved the way for the creation of the national parks, and 1949 was the landmark year in which the government passed an Act of Parliament to establish national parks to preserve and enhance their natural beauty and provide recreational opportunities for the public – the National Parks and Access to the Countryside Act. In 1951, the Peak District was the first area in the country to be designated as a national park, helping to protect and preserve it for the future.

Castleton - Andy & Susan Caffrey

Derbyshire Dialect

A

Abaht – about (as in *'abaht time'* – long overdue)
Afeered – afraid
Afore – before
Afters – the sweet course in a meal
Aggy – agitated
Agin – again, against
Aht – out (as in *'gone aht'* – gone out)
Ails – is wrong with (as in *'What ails thee?'* – What is wrong with you?)
Ale-house – pub
All along – always (as in *'I knew a wer reet all along'* – I was always convinced I was correct)
An' all – and all (as well)
Ankle-badger (or ankle-biter) – hanger-on, sponger
Apostle of the Peak – The Revd William Bagshawe, itinerant preacher

B

Back end – autumn, or late in the year (also Backendish – feels like autumn weather)
Back-scratcher – someone who seeks favour by behaving sycophantically
Backuds – backwards
Bad-mouth – criticise
Badging hook – large sickle

C

Can't spit sixpence – thirsty
Careerin' – rushing
Car'son – the village of Carsington
Cart off – take away
Cathedral of the Peak – parish church in the village of Tideswell
Causey – causeway or pavement

D

Derby Ram – Derbyshire's most

famous folk song
Derbyshire Neck – the disease of goitre
Derbyshire's Gretna Green – the village of Peak Forest

F

Faberry – gooseberry
Faff – mess about; dither; also **Faffy** – intricate, complicated
Fair to middlin' – keeping reasonably well (healthwise)
Fast – trapped (as in *'I'm stuck fast'* – I'm well and truly trapped)
Featherbed moss – peaty tracts on the uplands of the Dark Peak

H

Hug – a type of scrum in Ashbourne's football game (see 'Match of the Days' in Sports)
Husky-fusky – leapfrog
Hutch up – move along

L

Laddin' – courting (the female equivalent of wenchin')
Lapping – ladling
Larrop – eat greedily

O

Ower Bill's Mother's – in the distance (as in *'It's black ower Bill's mother's'* – it is likely to rain soon)
Ower t'wife's mother's – variation on the above

T

Tankered – exhausted
Tap dressing – alternative name for well dressing

V

Visitation of the Plague – when the Great Plague of 1665 came to Eyam from London (see the section on ghosts for more on this history).

Sacré Bleu

Below the surface of Treak Cliff (pronounced *'Trek Cliff'*), a steep hillside at the head of the Hope Valley, there is a unique deposit of fluorspar that is much

Ghost Stories
Tales of the Supernatural to Chill the Blood

Rattling Chains

A thirteenth-century stone sarcophagus was unearthed in Ashover's churchyard many years ago. Supposedly if you walk round it three times, then lie in it with your eyes closed, you will hear the ghostly sounds of rattling chains, although why anyone should want to do this is rather baffling.

Creepy Events at Calke Abbey

The faded splendour of Calke Abbey provides a unique insight into a fine baroque house which, like many country piles, stands on the site, and incorporates some of the fabric, of a medieval religious house of the Augustinian canons. Secularised in the reign of Henry VIII, any traces of earlier masonry have been disguised by rebuilding in 1701 and 1841, and apart from minor repairs and improvements in 1865, the introduction of the telephone in 1928 and electricity in 1962, this is the house where time has stood still.

When the mansion passed to the National Trust in 1985 it was in need of extensive repairs, but Calke Abbey was also ready to reveal its many

Calke Abbey - CC Oliver Mills

treasures and secrets. Excavating for drains and electricity cables on the east side of the house exposed not only the remains of the priory buildings, but five adult male skeletons dating from the twelfth to fourteenth centuries. They were laid in a strict east–west axis, which suggests they were the remains of the monastic occupants of Calke Priory, and although they are now buried in consecrated ground their ghosts have remained at Calke Abbey. Various members of staff and visitors have seen a hooded monk in the stable block. In the old brew house, a steward heard footsteps racing along the servants' passage and galloping up the stone stairs. The visiting family who emerged were all in shock. They had been walking along the servants' passage following an elderly man dressed in what they thought was a long, flowing coat, when he simply vanished before their eyes.

The eighteenth-century ticket and information office was originally the chop house where animal feed was prepared. Staff here have experienced being pinched and slapped, and on several occasions the wooden chairs used by visitors have been found next morning on the tables.

In the house itself, a steward saw a figure glide through the ground-floor lobby, but the most spiritually active area is the first floor of the east wing, which until about 1860 was one of the principal apartments of the house. Staff working in the rooms below have heard footsteps walk through these rooms, despite the fact no one was there. While closing the shutters in this wing, one member of staff felt a strange pressure build up, followed by the weight of a hand on his shoulder. Two spirit entities – believed to be NANNY PEARCE and LADY CAROLINE – have both shown themselves vividly. Visitors have reported seeing the elderly Nanny Pearce sitting watching them and have taken the lady in period dress seen in the boudoir to be an actor until they enquire and find no actors are circulating that day.

THE GHOSTS OF EYAM

It is hard to believe that the peaceful village of EYAM in the Peak District was once a place of terrible suffering and fear. But the village has a close and tragic association with the Great Plague of 1665. The people of Eyam made a courageous sacrifice which is thought to have saved cities in the north of England from the very worst of the terrible plague. Just 350 people lived in the village at the time of the plague in 1665. The local tailor received a parcel of cloth from London, which contained a horrible hidden secret… plague-carrying fleas. The tailor died a week later. It wasn't long before other villagers started dying too. While some locals wanted to leave quickly for Sheffield, their church leader urged them not to. He suggested that the entire village should shut itself in quarantine to prevent the spread of the plague. The villagers bravely agreed – even though they knew that it would mean certain death for most of them. Their courage paid off. They managed to reduce the spread of the plague, even though 260 out of the village's population of 350 died.

With such a dramatic history and scenes of human suffering, it is not surprising that Eyam is the source of some long-standing ghost stories. One of the best known is based at the plague cottages close to the church. One of these cottages is visited by a friendly-looking female ghost in a blue smock. While she has a pleasant demeanour, she has a habit of waking people up in the middle of the night. Another spot for otherworldly sightings is the local pub and B&B, the MINERS ARMS. Some stories recount how guests have occasionally left because they have had ghostly encounters. These include strange footsteps, doors slamming and even creepy giggling! Some say that these sounds are made by two of the village's plague victims, EMILY and SARAH. Other people claim to have seen an elderly lady dressed in black wandering the corridors. She is thought to be a former pub landlady who was murdered by her husband.

Eyam - iStock

Eyam Hall is an imposing Jacobean manor house which was built between 1671 and 1676. It is said to be haunted by the ghost of a servant girl who drowned in a well. She is not the only ghost of Eyam Hall. The spirit of an elderly man is reputed to spend a great deal of time in a specific room in the hall. Is it any wonder that the door to the room is now kept permanently locked?

Dickey's Skull

Screaming skulls are a very peculiar phenomenon, even by occult standards. Curiously, the occurrence of a disembodied human skull screaming, speaking or making its presence felt in other ways, is very much an English one. The Peak District has its own unnerving screaming skull story. The location for this strange tale, a building called Tunstead Farm near Chapel-en-le-Frith, is now so infamous that it is referred to by locals as Skull Farm. The farm is part of a very old hamlet. To find the origins of the story we must go all the way back to the 1790s. A writer who was visiting the farm was told by a man living there that the skull had been on the farm for around two centuries and that many people attested to seeing strange events associated with it. All remains quiet and calm – if the skull stays put. However, if anyone dares to move it, strange cries and screams are heard in the house.

The story of the skull gained particular prominence during the nineteenth century and remains well known to this day. There are a number of different theories about the origin of the skull. Because it is known by the name of Dickey, one of the theories runs that the skull was that of a soldier called Ned Dixon (shortened to Dickey) who was cruelly killed at the farm by his cousin after his return from fighting in a war. Poor Ned wanted to claim his rightful inheritance, but his cousin wasn't prepared to allow that to happen. Another theory runs that the skull was that of a woman who was murdered in the house. Prior to her death she was able to request that her body stay within the house for all time. Over the passing of the years her skeleton was lost and only her troubled skull remained. Yet another theory goes that the screaming skull belonged to a woman who had fallen in love with the same man as her sister. Her sister killed her and so, as she lay dying, she declared that her bones would not rest in any grave.

Whatever the true story of the skull's origins, it was associated with many odd occurrences. So great was its reputation that land owned by Tunstead Farm grew to be known as Dickey's Land. It was seen as the cause of strange events which took place when the London and North Western Railway Company attempted to build a railway bridge on land owned by Tunstead Farm. This would have created a link between Buxton and Whaley Bridge. Work started on the land, but it wasn't long until the new foundations started collapsing, with one part of the new bridge falling apart overnight! The railway company decided that they didn't want to take on the screaming skull any more. They made the decision to build further up the line instead. This fascinating story caused quite a stir and inspired the Lancashire dialect poet SAMUEL LAYCOCK to write a verse dedicated to the skull in 1870:

Address to Dickey

Neaw, Dickie, be quiet wi' thee, lad,

An' let navvies an' railways a' be;

Mon tha shouldn't do soa, its too bad,

What harm are they doin' to thee?

Deed folk shouldn't meddle at o'

But leov o' these matters to th'wick;

They'll see they're done gradely, aw know -

Dos' t' yer what aw say to thee, Dick?

The skull was reputed to be able to protect itself as well as its home. Another story goes that once, when the skull was stolen and taken to Disley, the thieves were terrified by weird noises and other phenomena which took place and quickly returned it to its rightful home.

Humour

We've just hired a fantastic cook from Derbyshire!

Bakewell?

Yes, and she does a lovely roast dinner too.

I bought a really comfy sofa in Derbyshire last week.

Chesterfield?

Well, it's more of a chaise longue actually.

A lad from Chaddesden was bragging to his mate: *'My computer beat me at chess, but it were no match for me at kick boxing.'*

How do you get a sweet old Derbyshire granny to swear?

Get another sweet old Derbyshire granny to shout 'BINGO!'

Derek and Duncan were long-time neighbours in Bolsover. Every time Derek saw Duncan coming round to his house, his heart sank. This was because he knew that, as always, Duncan would be visiting him in order to borrow something and he was fed up with it.

'I'm not going to let Duncan get away with it this time,' he said quietly to his wife, *'Watch what I'm about to do.'*

'Hi there, I wondered if you were thinking about using your hedge trimmer this afternoon?' asked Duncan.

'Oh, I'm very sorry,' said Derek, trying to look apologetic, 'but *I'm actually going to be using it all afternoon.'*

'In that case,' replied Duncan with a big grin, 'you won't be using your golf clubs, will you? Mind if I borrow them?'

HUMOUR

An elderly couple from Clay Cross are sitting at the dining table in their semi-detached house talking about making preparations for writing their wills. Bill says to his missus, Edna, *'I've been thinking, me duck, if I go first to meet me maker I don't want you to be on your own*

for too long. In fact, I think you could do worse than marry Colin in the chemist's or Dave with the fruit stall in the market. They'd provide for you and look after you when I'm gone.'

'That's very kind on you to think about me like that, Bill,' replies Edna, *'but I've already made my own arrangements!'*

A police officer was patrolling the lanes outside Matlock one night, when he noticed a car swerving all over the road. Quickly, he turned on his lights and siren and pulled the driver over. *'Sir, do you know you're all over the road? Please step out of the car.'*

When the man got out of the car, the policeman told him to walk in a straight line.

'I'd be happy to, offisher,' said the drunk, *'if you can just get the line to stop moving about.'*

A woman from Matlock called Moira was still not married at thirty-five and she was getting really tired of going to family weddings especially because her old Aunt Maud always came over and said, *'You're next!'*

It made Moira so annoyed, she racked her brains to figure out how to get Aunt Maud to stop. Soon after, an old uncle died and there was a big family funeral. Moira spotted Aunt Maud in the crematorium, walked over, pointed *at the coffin and said, with a big smile, 'You're next!'*

A man and his wife walked past a swanky new restaurant in Buxton. *'Did you smell that food?'* the woman asked. *'Wonderful!'*

Being the kind-hearted, generous man that he was, her husband thought, *'What the hell, I'll treat her!'*

So they walked past it a second time.

A Hooray Henry from Nottinghamshire was driving around Matlock in his fancy new car and realised that he was lost. The driver stopped a local character, old Tom, and said, *'Hey, you there! Old man, what happens if I turn left here?'*

'Don't know, sir,' replied Tom.

'Well, what if I turn right here – where will that take me?' continued the visitor.

'Don't know, sir,' replied old Tom.

Becoming exasperated, the driver continued, *'Well, what if I go straight on?'*

A flicker of knowledge passed over old Tom's face but then he replied, *'Don't know, sir.'*

'I say, old man, you don't know a lot, do you?' retorted the posh bloke.

Old Tom looked at him and said, *'I may not know a lot, sir, but I ain't lost like what you are!'* With that, old Tom walked off leaving the motorist stranded.

A man from Bakewell decided to become a monk so he went to the monastery and talked to the head monk.

The head monk said, *'You must take a vow of silence and can only say two words every three years.'*

The man agreed and after the first three years, the head monk came to him and said, *'What are your two words?'*

'Food cold!' the man replied.

Three more years went by and the head monk came to him and said, *'What are your two words?'*

'Robe dirty!' the man exclaimed.

Three more years went by and the head monk came to him and said, *'What are your two words?'*

'I quit!' said the man.

'Well,' the head monk replied, *'I'm not surprised. You've done nothing but complain ever since you got here!'*

Darren proudly drove his new convertible into Ashbourne and parked it on the main street. He was on his way to the charity shop to get rid of an unwanted gift, a foot spa, which he left on the back seat. He had walked halfway down the street when he realised that he had left the top down with the foot spa still in the back. He ran all the way back to his car, but it was too late… another five foot spas had been dumped in the car.

Local Names

Safer Driving

You might not think that the peaceful landscape of the Peak District would have much of an association with vehicle innovation, but you'd be wrong. In fact, one of the most famous British companies associated with vehicles is based in the area. FERODO is a British brake company based in CHAPEL-EN-LE-FRITH in High Peak. What is special about this local company is that it developed the very first modern brake friction materials, helping to make driving safer. It all started in the late 1890s when a man called HERBERT FROOD started manufacturing vehicle brakes in GORTON before moving the business to Chapel-en-le Frith in 1902.

Ferodo continues to be a leading manufacturer of high-performance automotive products, including braking systems, clutches, spark plugs and brake pads. As the company's website proudly reports, of the ten top-selling vehicles in Europe, Ferodo was fitted to eight of them.' Not bad for a small enterprise in the heart of the Peak District!

Clean Hands

Anyone who has ever needed to scrub heavy-duty oil and grime off their hands will probably be grateful to an inventor from DENBY, just outside the Peak District. This is because they created SWARFEGA, that well-known hand cleaner. It is made by Deb Limited, a company still based in Denby to this day. Wherever there is hard manual labour, Swarfega is to be found. It was invented back in the 1940s by an industrial chemist from HEANOR called AUDLEY BOWDLER WILLIAMSON. He set up a detergent-sales company, DEB SILKWARE PROTECTION LTD, and Swarfega became hugely popular. The company is still going strong.

One story goes that Swarfega was originally invented to extend the life of silk stockings, with the company name stemming from the word 'debutante'. When the emergence of nylon made the product look likely to become redundant, Williamson apparently suggested that mechanics had already found it useful for cleaning their hands. Whether or not this is just a clever marketing story, the product certainly provided a more effective and protective answer to mechanics and others than using harsh and potentially damaging products such as paraffin and petrol to wash their hands.

An Everyday Essential

We have a Peak District local to thank for protecting us from one of our most familiar foes – rain. It was Bradwell resident Samuel Fox, who produced the steel-ribbed collapsible umbrella which, though he developed it back in the 1800s, is very similar to the model we use today. In 1851, through his company, Fox Umbrella Frames Ltd, Fox developed what was called the 'Paragon' umbrella frame. His umbrella soon gained international fame.

One witty commentator said at the time:

'I should say that Mr. Fox had the Peak to thank for some of his commercial success. He was born in the Peak. There the rain-clouds are always gathering. What more natural than that Mr. Fox should turn his

the world's first successful collapsible umbrella frame, the true inventor was actually his friend and employee Joseph Hayward. Fox's company was entitled to all production rights and profits. So, next time you put up your umbrella against the rain, spare a thought for the Peak District local who first brought the collapsible umbrella to market.

attention to umbrellas? He was not one of the umbrella-making chiefs of Thibet, but he was the umbrella-making chief of the world – he was the world's friend, for his paragon frames have and do still shield people of all nations from the wet.'

However, while Samuel Fox made a great contribution to business and to helping the poor through his philanthropy, we should make a point for the sake of historical accuracy. For, although he is credited with inventing

Myths & Legends

Robin Hood

More commonly associated with Nottinghamshire, the mysterious figure of Robin Hood also has close mythical links with the Peak District.

The clues lie in the names dotted around the picturesque landscape of the Peaks. One of these is Robin Hood's Stride, an impressive stone crag set in stunning scenery. The story goes that Robin Hood walked across the entire breadth of the crag, adding even more powers to an already impressive legend! Robin Hood's Cave on Stanage Edge is said to have been used as a hideout by the hero.

Robin's faithful companion, Little John, or John Little, has an even stronger presence in the area, particularly in the village of Hathersage. In the village once stood a cottage said to be the house in which Little John lived out the last years of his life. In the local churchyard you can even find what is said to be John Little's headstone. As befits a man who was said to be very tall, the grave is very large! The inscription on the grave stone reads:

'Here lies buried Little John, the friend & lieutenant of Robin Hood. He died in a cottage (now destroyed) to the east of the churchyard. The grave is marked by this old headstone & footstone and is underneath this old yew tree.'

Of course no one knows for sure whether this really is the grave of

Little John. While the main headstone is relatively modern, there is an older one on the grave, though it is now impossible to read what it says. However, the owner of the nearby manor excavated the site in 1784 and did find an unusually large thighbone. It was reputed to have brought ill fortune on the area until it was reburied! While the bone is a compelling clue and there is much debate, we still have no definitive proof that Robin Hood and his band of merry men actually existed. But their legend continues to live on, in the Peak District and elsewhere.

The Stones of Mouselow

Just on the outer edge of the Peak District, in Glossop, is the location of a very weird story about a collection of stones. The Stones of Mouselow, as they are now known, were originally found at the site of Mouselow Castle on Mouselow Hill in Glossop. Being impressive stones with unusual markings, they were first incorporated into the wall of a house before being moved to the Buxton Museum. In the 1980s, the stones were taken back to Glossop as there was an archaeological dig on Mouselow Hill. The site was also excavated again. Here is where things get odd. The stones were about to be moved back to Buxton Museum and so were stored overnight in an office. Yet, when the staff returned the next day, they found that none of the computers in the office worked! No technician or logical explanation seemed to help. The staff brought other electrical equipment into the room and this also failed to work, supporting their theory that the stones were somehow preventing the computers from working. This idea was strengthened still further when the stones went back to Buxton and the computers began to work again! Some say that this effect is due to the stones' strong magnetic field. Others say it is because they are cursed! While their origins remain uncertain, their eerie reputation is now well established, and they are still to be found at Buxton Museum to this day.

The Mermaids of The Peak District

If legends are to be believed, two mermaids have made their home in the landlocked Peak District, a long way from the sea in any direction! The first is rumoured to live in what is known as MERMAID'S POOL, a body of water located below KINDER SCOUT. It is believed that Celtic water worship rituals took place here many years ago. One possible reason for this is because the water is salt water, which is very unusual for an inland lake. Another reason is because of a beautiful illusion that takes place at the nearby KINDER DOWNFALL waterfall which, when the wind is particularly strong, looks as if it is flowing upwards! The belief is that the water in the Mermaid's Pool has healing properties. Even better, the lake is also reputed to bring eternal life to those with the courage to pay it a visit at midnight at Easter! This is when the mermaid of the lake will appear. Visitors who meet with her approval will be granted immortal life. On the other hand, those who don't may be pulled down beneath the waters to die!

The Peak District's second mermaid is believed by some to reside in BLAKEMERE *(or Blake Meer)* POOL, a landlocked pool in a remote area of the Staffordshire Peak District. Two different legends have survived about this particular mermaid. In one version, she was brought to the area by a sailor from nearby THORNCLIFFE. Sadly, the sailor died and the mermaid, heartbroken and far from the sea, began to haunt Blakemere Pool. In a less romantic version of events, the story goes that a woman

Mermaid - iStock

rejected the approaches of a local man. So, in a fit of rage, he accused the woman of being a witch and very cruelly persuaded his fellow locals to drown her in the pool. The woman cursed the man with her last breath. Just a few days later, his corpse was discovered next to the pool, with his face covered in what looked like clawmarks! The woman is said to haunt the pool to this day as a mermaid with a dark side. It is said that even now, animals refuse to drink from the pool and birds refuse to fly over it!

The most recent recorded sighting of the terrifying apparition was in the nineteenth century when some locals worked hard to try do drain the lake. They were keen to find out if it was really bottomless, as it was reputed to be. However, when they began digging, the mermaid rose up from the lake and threatened that she would flood nearby LEEK and LEEKFRITH unless they stopped meddling with her lake, which they duly did!

Murder Mysteries: Peak District Murders

The Winster Duel

Dr Will Cuddie moved to Winster in Derbyshire when he was 27, having previously been a surgeon in the navy. He got on well with his patients, and was popular in the village.

He would give medical advice and treatment to the villagers, and did not charge a fee when the patient was from a poor family. One of his patients was Mary Brittlebank, the daughter of a wealthy local solicitor. Mary and William became friends, and found they were growing fonder of one another. They began 'walking out'.

Back in the early years of the nineteenth century, a solicitor was a professional man, but medicine was not regarded as a professional occupation. To the Brittlebank family, the Scottish doctor was not of high enough status to be romantically involved with their daughter. Mary's brothers decided that they would have to act to put a stop to the unacceptable liaison between their sister and the doctor.

One Monday afternoon in May 1821 the doctor was walking through the village, accompanied by Mary, when they were accosted by her brother, William. William Brittlebank demanded that his sister come with him immediately, and cease to

Bank House, the home of Dr Will Cuddie, in Winster. The fatal duel took place in the back garden

associate with Will Cuddie. The doctor responded in language that owed much to his previous life in the navy. The two men exchanged angry words and parted on very bad terms.

That same evening, Will received a letter from his sweetheart's brother, demanding satisfaction for the insults he had received during their argument. He told the doctor to name a time and place when the matter could be settled by a duel. He said that if the doctor refused to meet him he would publicly denounce him as a coward.

Will Cuddie regarded the whole thing as preposterous, and ignored the letter, but he received a second written challenge the next morning. Again, the doctor ignored the foolish message. However, later that day, William Brittlebank turned up at Dr Cuddie's house, accompanied by his brothers FRANCIS and ANDREW and a friend, EDMUND SPENCER. Spencer went into the house and informed the young doctor that he must either apologise to William Brittlebank or fight a duel.

Will refused, but Spencer insisted. Reluctantly, the doctor agreed and went out into his garden, where the Brittlebank brothers were waiting. They had two loaded pistols with them. William took one and the doctor the other. William walked 15 yards, then turned and fired. Will Cuddie was shot in the abdomen, the bullet having lodged in his bowels. He died of his wound the next afternoon.

The village was outraged at the killing. The doctor had not wanted to fight a duel and had been coerced into it. They were even more outraged when a handwritten letter from Mary Brittlebank was found in Will's pocket after his death. In it she warned him to keep out of the way of her family 'as they are quite bent on shooting'. A rumour spread that only one of the duelling pistols had been loaded. It was whispered that the gun given to Dr Cuddie had been empty, though those present at the duel continued to claim that he had fired and missed.

An inquest found that the popular 31-year-old doctor had died through wilful murder. The brother who had fired the shot fled. Despite a £100 price on his head, he escaped to Australia, where he remained for the rest of his life. His other two brothers, Francis and Andrew, were tried for the murder along with Edmund Spencer, but were acquitted.

The Winnats Pass Murders

At one time, Peak Forest in Derbyshire was the primary destination for lovers who wanted to get married without the consent of their parents.

The fact that the local chapel lay inside the boundaries of the royal forest meant that the priest could marry couples immediately without the need for banns. It was a fast, no-questions-asked ceremony, but owing to an anomaly in the law it was legal and binding. It was Derbyshire's own GRETNA GREEN. Not surprisingly, many couples made their way to PEAK FOREST. The Marriage Act of 1753 should have put an end to the practice, but it continued on a lesser scale. The last couple married there in this way was as late as 1938.

One such couple who decided to travel there were ALAN and CLARA. Clara was from a wealthy family. Although Alan was from a good family, they were much poorer. Clara's parents had disapproved of the match and forbidden Clara to see her young man. The two decided to elope, and to head for Peak Forest where they could be married without the consent of her father.

It was April 1758 when they set out on horseback. When they reached CASTLETON, they called in at an inn to rest and to ask for directions. There they were observed by a boisterous quartet of local lead miners – JOHN BRADSHAW, NICK COOK, TOM HALL and FRANK BUTLER – who were drinking in the bar. The men quietened down and eavesdropped as the landlord gave the couple directions, advising them to head down WINNATS PASS, a rocky ravine just a mile or so along the road. The men noticed the good clothes that the strangers were wearing, and speculated that they might be carrying a large amount of money. When the couple went into another room to eat a meal, the four young miners resumed their drinking, getting so rowdy that the landlord eventually threw them out.

This was an era when strangers were looked on with suspicion and mistrust, and as a possible source of ill-gotten gains for those who were not averse to violent crime. These 'strangers' need not be from distant parts; they could just as easily be from a town a few miles away or a village just up the road. They were not from Castleton, so they were foreign. It was a very parochial time.

The four men decided to wait for the young lovers to set out again on their journey and to waylay them. They picked up a fifth man, JIM ASHTON, and armed themselves with pickaxe handles. They headed for Winnats Pass and there they waited. After an hour or so, they saw Alan and Clara riding into the rocky ravine. Yelling and cursing, they leapt out and pulled the man and girl from their horses, which quickly bolted back towards Castleton. The men roughly searched Alan and Clara, and shouted with delight when they discovered that they were carrying no less than £200.

The terrified couple were pushed into a barn, while the lead miners discussed what they could do with this newly acquired fortune of £40 each. When the men re-entered the barn, Alan begged them to spare his and Clara's lives, but the men just stared at him without speaking. Realising that the men would not show any mercy, Alan hurled himself at them. His reward was to be clubbed to death. Clara watched in horror as her lover died, and then suffered the same fate. The men left the two dead bodies in the barn overnight, but the next day they

Winnats Pass • Andy & Susan Caffrey

disposed of them by throwing them down a disused mine shaft nearby. When the riderless horses arrived back in Castleton, it was realised that the young couple had perished, but the exact method of their death was not known.

The murderers did not enjoy their new wealth. A year after the brutal murders, John Bradshaw met an early death, being killed by falling rocks, and Nicholas Cook died when he fell from a buttress. Both of these accidents occurred in Winnats Pass, which raises issues of ironic justice and the possibility of the very rocks themselves wreaking revenge on the guilty men. Tom Hall and Frank Butler found the knowledge of what they had done too much to bear, the former committing suicide and the latter going insane. The fifth man – Jim Ashton – used his share of the loot to go into the horse-trading business, but without success. All his horses fell ill and died. It was Ashton who left a deathbed confession to the robbery and murders, naming the others as his partners in crime.

The skeletons of the murdered lovers were discovered ten years after the crime, and they were interred in St Edmund's churchyard in Castleton. The red Morocco leather saddle from Clara's horse can be seen on display in the little museum in the entrance of Speedwell Cavern.

Speedwell Cavern - Andy & Susan Caffrey

Sport

The Peak District is often packed full of people enjoying sporting and outdoor activities. Walking is of course one of the most popular of these.

With so many stunning sites (and sights), you'll never go short of somewhere to walk in the Peaks. Whether it is a relaxing stroll or a hardcore hike, you'll be able to enjoy it in this beautiful area. Walkers can choose from national or local trails or explore over 200 square miles (524 sq km) of open access land or 1,867 miles (3,000km) of rights of way. The PEAK DISTRICT NATIONAL PARK website highlights the following as good walks:

For experienced walkers, the long-distance 431km (268 miles) PENNINE WAY NATIONAL TRAIL follows the Pennine chain along the rugged backbone of England from Edale crossing Kinder Scout, the highest point in the Peak District at 636 metres (2,087ft).

THE TRANS PENNINE TRAIL is part of the E8 European Walking Route, connecting the National Park to the Turkish border – a walk of 4,023km (2,500 miles). The beautiful LIMESTONE WAY is 74km (46 miles) through delightful limestone scenery.

The DERWENT VALLEY HERITAGE WAY is 88km (55 miles) long and weaves through some of the area's richest natural landscape and industrial heritage, given recognition as a World Heritage Site.

Walking in the Peak District - iStock Nico_65

Climbing

The landscape of the Peak District also lends itself very naturally to the sport of rock climbing. The area is known for having some of the most demanding climbing routes in Europe, such as STANAGE EDGE near Sheffield and the ROACHES in the Staffordshire Moorlands. There are so many recorded climbs in the Peaks that nobody knows quite how many there are! But apparently, they exceed 10,000...

The Roaches - Andy & Susan Caffrey

Stanage Edge - Andy & Susan Caffrey

Match of the Days

Ashbourne's Royal Shrovetide ('Shrovie') football match is no ordinary game of soccer. The goalposts are three miles apart and the pitch is two miles wide; there is no limit to the number of players and the 'pitch' is the shopping streets, 'gennels', streams and culverts of the town. Needless to say, all the shopkeepers nail large protective boards to the front of their premises throughout Shrovetide to prevent damage during the rough-and-tumble of the match.

The game is contested between the *Up'ards* (people who live on the north side of Henmore Brook) and the *Down'ards* (people who live on the south side) and the two teams inevitably find themselves splashing around in the brook at some stage during the match.

Play takes place between 2pm and 10pm on Shrove Tuesday and Ash Wednesday. Other than a prohibition on carrying the ball in a bag, a ban on murder and a discouragement of 'unnecessary violence', there are virtually no restrictions on the way the ball can be grabbed from an opponent or moved around. This type of free-for-all football is known as hugball, because it proceeds in a series of scrums, or hugs, which make a rugby scrum seem like child's play.

Turning up, which starts the game at 2pm on Shrove Tuesday, is carried out by a guest of honour, who throws the ball into the air. The event achieved 'royal' status in 1928, when the Prince of Wales turned up the ball and is said to have ended up with a cut on his head. PRINCE CHARLES had the honour in 2003, but escaped without injury.

Scoring, or goaling, is achieved when a player hits the ball three times against the 'goalpost', or marker board, at one end of the pitch. If a goal is scored after 6pm, play ends for that day, but if goaling takes place before 6pm, a new ball is turned up and play begins again.

New balls are made each year and painted with designs appropriate to the celebrity who turns up the ball. The game originated in Elizabethan times and some historians believe that the very first ball was the severed head of a man who had been executed!

'Tis a Glorious Game

Anyone who believes that football anthems are a modern phenomenon should think again. Ashbourne's famous Royal Shrovetide Football Match is always preceded by a pre-game luncheon and the singing of an anthem, which was composed in 1891:

There's a town still plays this glorious game
Tho 'tis but a little spot
And year by year the contest's fought
From the field that's called Shaw Croft
Then friend meets friend in friendly strife
The leather for to gain
And they play the Game right manfully,
In snow, sunshine or rain

Chorus:
'Tis a glorious game, deny it who can
That has the pluck of an Englishman

Second Verse:
For a loyal the Game shall ever be
No matter when or where,
And treat that Game as ought but free
Is more than the boldest dare
Through the ups and downs of its
chequered life
May the ball still ever roll,
Until by fair and gallant strife
We've reached the treasur'd goal.

Ashbourne's Royal Shrovetide Football Match may be somewhat rougher than games played under the rules of Association Football, but its song is rather less aggressive and a good deal more sporting than those heard on the terraces of many Premiership clubs!

Ashbourne's Royal Shrovetide Football Match
iStock - Mikedabell

Local Recipes

High Peak Lamb Cobbler

SERVES 4

This traditional, wholesome, rustic stew is best made with lamb bred in a handful of farms in Derbyshire's glorious High Peak. Like most stews, this dish benefits from long cooking. Serve with floury or mashed potatoes, minted peas and a pile of pickled red cabbage.

Ingredients:

- 1 onion, finely sliced
- 1 clove garlic, crushed
- 1 large leek, chopped and washed
- 1 small turnip, diced
- 2 tsp rosemary, chopped
- 1 tsp parsley, chopped
- 1 tsp thyme, chopped
- 1 tsp oregano, chopped
- Sea salt
- Freshly ground black pepper
- 900g diced shoulder of lamb
- 1 litre stock (or use Marigold Bouillon or Kallo stock cubes)
- 28g pearl barley
- 28g plain flour, seasoned with salt & pepper
- Oil for frying

Method:

In a large saucepan, warm some vegetable oil and add all the vegetables. Cook gently until they're transparent then add the herbs.

While this is sweating, toss the diced lamb in the seasoned flour and fry briskly in batches in another pan, until it's browned. Add the vegetables to the meat, plus the pearl barley and mix thoroughly. Add the stock and seasoning. Stir well and cover.

Simmer for about 1½ hours, until the meat is tender.

High Peak Lamb Cobbler / iStock

Bakewell Pudding

Ingredients:

500g ready-made puff pastry

5 tbsp seedless raspberry jam

100g unsalted butter

100g caster sugar

5 eggs

150g ground almonds

Almond essence

The first thing to say is that there are puddings and tarts; Bakewell is famous for both but they're quite different. Legend has it that the pudding originated as a result of a mistake made by a cook at a local inn, but there's little proof of this. The earliest recipe given by Eliza Acton in 1845 is essentially an inch thick, rich custard of egg yolks, butter, sugar and ratafia (almond essence) poured over a layer of jam and candied peel. Mrs Beeton had a recipe which omitted the peel and included ground almonds in the custard – a version much nearer to the one we enjoy today. The actual recipe is a trade secret, but this comes close.

© Bakewell Pudding Shop 2013

Method:

Preheat the oven to 375°F/190°C/Gas 5. Roll the pastry onto a lightly floured surface to form a circle a few inches larger than the tart tin. Carefully spread the jam evenly over the pastry base.

In a large mixing bowl, cream together the butter and sugar until pale and fluffy. Add the eggs one by one, beating well each time. Stir in equal amounts of the ground almonds after you've added the egg, stirring well until combined. Continue until all the eggs and ground almonds are used up then stir in the almond essence.

Pour the filling mixture into the pastry case and gently spread it evenly over the jam. Bake in the middle of the oven for 35-40 minutes until the surface is golden brown.

Dust with icing sugar once it's cooled and serve with a dollop of double cream.

Buxton Pudding

This simple, tasty pudding was a great way of using up stale cake or bread and is still served in cafes in Buxton; in years gone by, farmers' wives would have taken it out into the fields for their hay-making husbands to eat by the slice! Serve piping hot with custard or cold – a slice goes beautifully with a cuppa. Make the pastry base by all means, but ready-made will do nicely.

Ingredients:

Packet of ready-made shortcrust pastry

For the Filling:

100g softened butter

100g caster sugar

2 medium eggs

150g plain cake crumbs (Madeira cake works well)

4 tbsp strawberry jam, gently warmed through

Method:

Preheat the oven to 375°F/190°C/Gas 5.

Roll the pastry out on a lightly floured work top to about 5mm thick. Line an 18cm flan dish with the pastry and spread the warmed jam over the base.

In a mixing bowl cream together the softened butter and caster sugar. Add the beaten eggs gradually then fold in the cake crumbs.

Put the mixture on top of the jam in the pastry case, spreading it out evenly. Sprinkle over a little caster sugar. Put the flan on a baking tray in the oven for about 25 minutes. When golden and baked through, remove. Eat it either hot with custard or cold with a cuppa.

Derbyshire Lobby

Lobby is a sort of hotpot – a dish made traditionally with salted or cured beef, onion and potato. Its origins are thought to be traced from North Staffordshire although it's commonplace throughout the country. In Derbyshire it was eaten by working people, mainly farmers and potters who couldn't afford the more expensive cuts of meat. All sorts of ingredients would have been thrown in including pig's trotters and offal. This contemporary recipe still makes use of cheaper cuts of meat – add the trotters if you want to be old school! At home we'd have this on pancakes; Mum always made lots of batter and we had the meat on the first one, then ate the second sprinkled with sugar and half an orange squeezed over it.

Ingredients:

450g stewing or braising steak, fat removed and cut into small chunks

Generous slug of vegetable oil

1 medium white onion, finely chopped

4 large potatoes, diced

1 swede, diced

4 celery sticks, chopped

4 carrots, chopped

Pearl barley

1 litre stock (or use Marigold Bouillon or Kallo stock cubes)

Sea salt

4 bay leaves

Freshly ground black pepper

Splash of malt vinegar (optional, but many Derbyshire cooks say this is an essential addition)

Basic pancake batter

115g plain or self-raising flour

Pinch of salt

1 egg

280ml milk

Method:

Heat the vegetable oil in a large pan. Add the onion and cook gently for 10 minutes until it's transparent but not browned. Add the carrot, celery and swede and cook for a further 10 minutes.

Remove the vegetables from the pan and put into a casserole pot – one with a lid. Heat another slug of oil in the pan and flash-fry the meat, sealing it. Add to the casserole along with the stock, barley, bay leaves and seasoning.

Cook in a medium hot oven for a couple of hours – the longer and slower you can cook it, the better.

For the pancakes, sift the flour and salt together. Add the lightly beaten egg. Add the milk gradually then beat with a whisk until you've got a creamy batter the consistency of single cream.

Heat a teaspoon of vegetable oil in a frying pan – when the fat's smoking hot, add a ladle of the batter. Turn the pancake after about 3 minutes and cook the other side – it should be starting to brown (I used to love the crispy bits round the edges!).

Local Customs

WELL DRESSED

A thanksgiving for a supply of pure water during the Black Death? An expression of gratitude for a productive well in a period of drought? A pagan ceremony which was hijacked by Christians? The origin of the Peak District tradition of well dressing is uncertain, but the practice of decorating wells with pictures made from petals pressed onto damp clay is commonly believed to have begun about 650 years ago in the village of TISSINGTON.

It is known that Tissington suffered from an outbreak of the Black Death in 1348, and the first dressings may well have been a thanksgiving for the end of that terrible epidemic. Over the ensuing years, the custom spread to many other settlements in the White Peak. However, YOULGREAVE'S first dressings did not appear until 1829, when they were created to celebrate the arrival of the first piped water in the village – hence the local name of tap dressings.

Well dressing has its own rituals and its own language. The pictures are drawn on a large sheet of paper and then transferred to the surface of a bed of damp clay by 'pricking' their outlines through the paper with a pin or a needle. The next stage is 'petalling', which involves filling in the spaces between the outlines by pressing petals and other natural materials, such as leaves, bark and stones, onto the clay.

Well Dressing at Tissington - Andy & Susan Caffrey

To avoid everything falling out when the completed picture is hoisted to a vertical position and put on display, the clay is contained in a wooden frame and held in place by nails protruding from the base. Before it can be used, the clay has to be thoroughly mixed with water in a process known as 'puddling'. This is achieved by a puddler, suitably clad in Wellington boots, standing in a large metal bath and tramping around in the mixture for some considerable time.

Puddling is no longer practised in many villages, because an enterprising firm in Stoke-on-Trent has tapped a lucrative market by selling clay that has already been puddled, thereby striking a blow to tradition, but sparing well-dressers a great deal of soggy labour!

On the Right Lines?

When the people of Chapel-en-le-Frith decided to try their hand at well dressing for the first time in 1995, they sought the advice of an experienced well-dresser, particularly on the vexed subject of outlining.

The dressers of Tissington have always maintained that shapes within the pictures should be outlined to create definition. In some villages this is achieved by using rows of coffee beans, while other places employ threads of black wool, but Chapel-en-le-Frith's adviser was of a different persuasion.

He said, *'None o' t' best artists use outlining in their pictures, nor should thee. Tuck t'petals into t'clay around each o' t' shapes and tha'll find that yer picture'll be as clear as day.'*

The dressers decided that they would heed this advice for some of the shapes in their composition, but use cloves to outline less distinct parts of their picture. Over the next day, they watched in horror as oil from the cloves ran into neighbouring petals and discoloured them.

After debating whether they could pass off the effects of this disaster as artistic licence, the dressers realised that they would have to unpick their work and start all over again, being careful to use coffee beans rather than cloves in their second attempt.

When they had completed their picture, the proud dressers decided to invite their adviser to inspect their handiwork. Hoping for some positive strokes, they awaited his verdict. After careful perusal, he said, *'It's not reet bad for a first effort.'*

Undeterred by being damned with faint praise, the people of Chapel-en-le-Frith have continued to produce annual well dressings, but they have never again used cloves!

SAYING IT WITH PAPER FLOWERS

Ashford-in-the-Water is a pretty place in a beautiful setting on the north bank of the River Wye. The village is known for its sheep-wash enclosure, its picturesque three-arched bridge, its wells and its church, which is modest in size but contains some remarkable monuments.

Above the entrance porch there is a Norman tympanum with a carving of two animals separated by a tree. Although the identity of the two creatures is not clear, the animal on the left could be a hog or wild boar and that on the right could be a wolf. Some historians believe that the

Ashford in the Water - IStock

carving depicts the Royal Forest of the Peak, a hunting reserve for the Norman kings, which covered vast swathes of north-west Derbyshire.

The church's other notable survivals hang from the roof of the north aisle. These are four 'maidens' garlands', or 'virgins' crants', each of which was hung in the church after being carried in the funeral procession of a betrothed young woman who had died before her wedding day. The garlands have white paper roses attached to a wooden frame, together with a glove or handkerchief which belonged to the young lady.

Originally there were seven garlands, but two had been lost by 1900 and another fell from the roof and broke in 1935. The four remaining garlands were cleaned and restored in 1987 before being re-hung with protective Perspex covers.

The practice of hanging maidens' garlands died out at the beginning of the nineteenth century, with Ashford's most recent virgin's crant dating from 1801. Perhaps there has been a lack of suitable subjects since that time!

Saying it with Wild Flowers

May 29th (Charles II's birthday) was declared a national holiday in 1660, with parliament ordering it to be kept as an annual day of thanksgiving for the restoration of the monarchy. It was known as Oak Apple Day in commemoration of the King's escape from Cromwell's forces by hiding in an oak tree near Boscobel House.

Celebrations took place on this special occasion in towns and villages throughout the country until the holiday was abolished in 1859. Despite the removal of official recognition for Oak Apple Day, the village of Castleton has maintained an annual commemoration with its unique Garlanding Ceremony.

A local man is dressed as Charles II and a huge conical garland of wild flowers is placed over his head and upper body. Accompanied by a local lady dressed as his consort, a troupe of dancers and a band, the 'King' is paraded around the village on horseback, with the procession pausing at each of Castleton's six hostelries for 'refreshment'.

At the end of this pub crawl, the 'King' is relieved of his enormous garland, which is then hoisted to the pinnacle of the church tower. Needless to say, the procession attracts many followers!

Castleton - Andy & Susan Caffrey

Famous Locals

FLORENCE NIGHTINGALE

The 'Lady with the Lamp' is one of the Peak District's most famous former residents. While she was born in Florence, the city from which she took her name, Florence Nightingale's family later moved to the UK to a home they had built in the Peak District. The house in Matlock was called Lea Hurst and was to become a summer home for Florence for the rest of her life. Florence Nightingale was a vital figure in helping to organise the care of wounded soldiers during the Crimean War. Her rigorous approach to ward and patient care meant that many more of the dangerously ill soldiers survived. Her influence lives on to this day as she established the first professional training school for nurses, the Nightingale Training School at St Thomas's Hospital, and published many reports and books on nursing. Nightingale not only shaped nursing, but also significantly influenced the design of wards and the control of infection and many other aspects vital to improving patient care.

She also established a school of midwifery nursing at King's College Hospital which, like her approach to nursing, provides a model to this day. Among her many well-deserved honours, Nightingale was the inspiration behind the founding of the International Red Cross.

Florence Nightingale - iStock

Dame Vivienne Westwood

You probably wouldn't associate a small village in the High Peak with one of the most influential figures in punk and fashion. But, up until the age of 14, Vivienne Westwood (her surname was Swire back then) called pretty Tintwistle home. History doesn't record whether she took part in the traditional well-dressing ritual that is held in the old part of the village every year. But it does record how this Peak District local made good by becoming one of the biggest names in British fashion. She is credited with bringing the edginess of punk into mainstream fashion. It was her clothing design for Malcolm McLaren's infamous 'Sex' clothing boutique which garnered public attention. Westwood grew her

collection of four shops in London into a network of high-end stores across the world. She is recognised as one of the most inflential fashion designers, with collections such as *Cut and Slash* and the *Red Label*. Westwood was awarded an OBE in 1992.

Dame Ellen MacArthur

Another Dame with Peak District roots, Dame Ellen MacArthur, who hails originally from Whatstandwell, near Matlock, is famous for sailing as a solo long-distance yachtswoman. MacArthur broke the world record for the fastest solo circumnavigation of the globe in 2005. The first time that she gained public attention was in 2001, when she gained second place in the Vendée Globe solo round-the-world sailing race. Following this, MacArthur was appointed a Member of the Order of the British Empire (MBE) for services to sport. She was the youngest person to complete the voyage, being only 24. Now retired, MacArthur runs the organisations she created, the Ellen MacArthur Foundation, a charity that works with businesses and education to speed up the transition to a circular economy and the Ellen MacArthur Cancer Trust, a charity that takes young people sailing to help them regain their confidence as they recover from cancer.

Dame Hilary Mantel

The town of Hadfield, which is located to the south of the River Etherow, on the border between Derbyshire and Greater Manchester, was the place where acclaimed author, Hilary Mantel, another Peak District Dame, grew up. The mill town was home to this writer who has won the Man Booker prize not once, but twice. Mantel is acclaimed for her captivating historical novels. Her novel *Wolf Hall*, the first in a trilogy, was made into a BBC drama in 2015 and then turned into a stage play performed by the Royal Shakespeare Company. The second book of the trilogy, *Bring Up The Bodies*, was also made into a successful stage play. Her novel *Fludd*, set in a mill village in the north of England, was awarded the Winifred Holtby Memorial Prize, the Cheltenham Prize and the Southern Arts Literature Prize. Her 2006 novel *Beyond Black* was shortlisted for a Commonwealth Writers Prize and the 2006 Orange Prize for Fiction. Mantel was awarded a CBE in 2006. Hadfield is also famous for being the filming location for much of weird and wonderful television series, *The League of Gentlemen*, and special 20th anniversary episodes of the series were recently filmed in the area.

TESS DALY

Tess Daly is a familiar face to anyone who watches television. She is probably best known for being a presenter on Strictly Come Dancing.

Daly, who worked as a model before moving on to TV fame, grew up in Birch Vale, a village in the High Peak district of Derbyshire. Daly is also an author, having penned two novels, *The Camera Never Lies* and *It's Up To You New York*.

TIMOTHY DALTON

The peaceful world of Derbyshire has a close association with the 'shaken, not stirred' world of James Bond.

That's because Timothy Dalton, James Bond star of *The Living Daylights* and *Licence to Kill*, grew up in Belper in Derbyshire. While best known for his role in the suave spy's history, this local man is also famous for roles in *Jane Eyre, Hot Fuzz* and *Penny Dreadful*.

Biography

Camilla Zajac is an author and copywriter who wrangles with words for publishers and companies in sectors as varied as engineering, telematics and manufacturing. Camilla goes to the Peak District for the healthy, invigorating walks and stays for the tea and cake.

Find out more at:
www.greenlightcopywriting.co.uk